COLLEGE

CONFIDENTIAL

— The College Handbook —

An Insider's Guide to Success

—M. Doss Winter—

Snowshoe Press LLC, 107 South Broadway, Suite 217, Riverton WY
82501

Dedication

This book is dedicated first and foremost to my Lord and Savior because without Him I can achieve nothing. This book is also dedicated to my amazing parents, Bill and Michelle, who have always been there to support, guide, and help me through everything in life. Without them none of this was possible. Lastly, I want to dedicate this book to my younger brother Sam. I hope this book will help him in his journey.

About the Book

College Confidential is a survival guide written BY a college student FOR college students, with a focus on traditionally aged incoming freshmen. It was written with the intention of helping future students avoid and overcome some of the obstacles that the author faced while in college.

The author discloses the secret to success, which ultimately boils down to helping the reader to work through the obstacles that lay in front of him or her.

College Confidential solves "how to" mysteries including: how to study effectively; how to score points with a professor; how to deal with an unruly roommate; how to handle a drinking culture; how to manage a tight budget; how to avoid landlord troubles; and how to stay mentally and physically fit.

College will be an extraordinary time in your life. You will be faced with many new and different challenges that you haven't been confronted with before. The author argues from personal experience that nothing positive comes from avoiding these issues. *College Confidential* gives you the tips you need to deal with the inevitable challenges you will face. *College Confidential* promises to help you become a stronger, smarter, and more confident student, ready to take on the trials of higher education.

College Confidential will guide you during your collegiate journey to help you become the person you truly want to be!

Table of Contents

Introduction

So you're now on your own. Finally! Your teenage years are soon ending, and the journey into adulthood is fast approaching. Your college education is upon you and the world is in front of you. This is a time of huge change and it can be quite a culture shock. It is a time that evokes varied and sometimes conflicting emotions – excitement, dread, adventure, responsibility. The peaks are high but the valleys are just as low. College can be a confusing and challenging time. No fear, I am here to help!

As a seasoned college student myself, I know just what you will be going through and I understand the challenges you will face. I am here to give you the inside scoop on how you can avoid the problems that may come your way so that you can get the most out of your college experience. No matter where you go to school, these tips are meant to guide you along the way. College should be the best time of your life. After all, you are on your own and you have more freedom than you have ever had before. There are so many opportunities out there, and the world is yours to explore and thrive in! You CAN make this an AMAZING time. But remember, a CAPSLOCKED AMAZING doesn't happen by accident. I am here to help make AMAZING happen for you.

There are many aspects that make up your new college life. These include new living arrangements, roommates, going to classes, trying not to starve, meeting new people, learning to study, going to parties, living on a budget, staying healthy, trying to discover what you want to do for the rest of your life, and the overall experience of growing up. All of these things piling on you at once can feel quite overwhelming.

As a veteran college student myself I am going to teach you certain "tricks of the trade" I have learned along the way that will help you tackle each of these problems. Many people seem to forget the basics that can save them from a world of hurt. A lot of things I experienced I learned the hard way. Hopefully you can learn early on in your college career to not make the same mistakes. By avoiding these mistakes you will definitely save a lot of time, a fair amount of trouble, and future headaches.

In the first section I will help you out with a few tips to give you an edge in a category that too many people neglect once they are on their own, Personal Health.

1   Personal Health

The thing about personal health issues is that they can seem insignificant at first but they can turn into big problems later if you ignore warning signs. Oftentimes important health issues can be pushed aside or even completely forgotten in the strange and busy new life you are now leading. Most likely your parents will not be there to tell you to do the important things that need to be done during this new lifestyle change. Where students get into trouble is when they disregard even the most basic health practices, and the consequences of this are very real and eventually inevitable. The two most important areas of personal health you need to focus on are your mental health and your physical health.

Life in the Asylum

The key to staying sane and grounded in your now upside down world is to be mentally healthy. By being mentally healthy I am not talking about how to deal with an actual mental disorder. I am talking about staying happy, and keeping your emotions in check, so that you're able to learn. With all the drastic lifestyle changes you will go through this can sometimes be difficult to do but this is a must. The once lost but now famous saying "Keep Calm and Carry On" presents a simple but profound truth.

The biggest key to being mentally strong in college is to minimize the bad times and maximize the good times. Work through your bad feelings quickly and learn how to generate the good feelings you need. An old pitching coach of mine used to tell me to always "have a short memory." The thought is to forget about what happened in the previous pitch and to not worry about the next pitch. You can't do anything about those pitches and you need to focus all your energy on the present pitch so that you can throw it with maximum effort. This is often referred to as "living in the moment" or "maximizing the now". It is easy to say, but you may be asking "how do I do this?" Here are a few actions that you can take…

Find Your Happy Place

For many of you college can be a life-altering event and because of the numerous changes that occur, can be very stressful. So how should you fight stress? Simple; with de-stressor activities. Find something to take your mind off of the things that stress you out. Examples of popular de-stressors are: yoga, running, listening to music, writing in a journal, reading, cooking, meditation, and prayer. Your de-stressors are personal because everyone is wired differently mentally.

Your main goal is to find something that makes YOU happy and that can relieve YOUR stress. When you find something that works for you personally, make it a routine. Do whatever it may be at least a couple of times a week, or whenever you are feeling overwhelmed. But, don't go overboard here. Let's say that your de-stressor activity is playing video games with your friends. Go ahead and kill zombies for an hour if it makes you feel better, but don't find yourself up at 3:00 A.M. on the verge of a Mountain Dew induced sugar coma after 8 straight hours in front of the T.V.

This will only make your life worse and I guarantee that it will not decrease the stress in your life!

Aside from personal de-stressors, there are also universal de-stressors. One of them is laughter. Being able to laugh is ridiculously beneficial to your mental health and is something we should all do a bit more often. Hormones that cause stress such as cortisol, epinephrine, and dopamine are reduced by laughter. In

> **Reminders -**
> *A universal de-stressor is laughter. Much research has shown that laughter is quite beneficial to both your physical and mental health.*

addition to reducing stress causing hormones, laughing can also raise levels of beneficial hormones like endorphins and neurotransmitters.[1] So, remember to laugh it up every chance you get!

Don't Forget About the "Little People"

What I mean by this is that we all have certain people in our life, whomever they may be - moms, dads, siblings,

---

[1] Scott, Elizabeth. "The Stress Management and Health Benefits of Laughter." About.com. 18 June 2012. 12 December 2012.
http://stress.about.com/od/stresshealth/a/laughter.htm

grandparents, or special friends - that are close to us and who have had a profound impact on who we are. Even though you are on your own now, these people should not be forgotten because they were, and are, the backbone to your mental health.

With a new and hectic schedule it can be easy to take these people for granted and overlook all of the contributions that they have made to your life. Make sure to have regular contact with this support system. Fortunately our modern society is so full of ways to stay in touch with anybody, anywhere, anytime it is pretty much impossible to not have an easily accessible communication device at hand.

At the minimum of once a week you should call, text, Skype (or whatever else your personal preference may be) the members of your support system. My favorite time to do this is on a Sunday afternoon or evening. This is when I, as most people, have some down time. Chatting with my

> **Quick Tip –**
> *For an extra mental refill, if possible, try to see your loved ones in person.*

support team helps me catch up with my loved ones, it relieves my stress, and it re-energizes me mentally for the upcoming week.

Flying High by Staying Grounded

A great mental health success tip is to find a way to stay as level headed and grounded as possible. There will be many highs and lows throughout your college career and trying to stay as even-keeled as possible is a huge advantage. Never let your highs get too high or your lows get too low. Always remember that your circumstances, whatever they may be, can completely change 180 degrees in a moment's notice.

One way many people help to keep themselves grounded is by attending religious services. Oftentimes one's faith is a driving force behind one's thoughts, feelings, and actions. If you are religious I would recommend finding a place where you can practice your religion and feed your spiritual nature. If you are not religious I still recommend that you find other activities that work for you personally to keep you calm, stable, and level-headed. Remember "Meditation beats Medication" every time.

Kipling's poem about "Keeping your head when all about you are losing theirs..." is good advice, but being able to do takes practice.

Physically Fit

We all know that the mind is the most important part of our body, it being at the center of every thought, word, and deed that comes to us and from us. But being physically healthy in college is of vital importance as well, and is something that quite a few people overlook and they do so at their own peril.

You will experience a wealth of new freedom in every aspect of your life. Unfortunately, many students misuse this freedom and often ignore their bodies' needs. Have you ever heard of the freshman 15? As in putting on an extra 15 lbs. during your freshman year? There is a reason that this saying exists. It can be quite a shock when you look in the mirror after a month or two of eating whatever you want with no thought of the consequences. You see round places where once there were flat places!

When people disregard what they put in their mouths during some or all of their college years, it can be disastrous for their body, not only appearance-wise but medically speaking as well. These next tips will seem basic but they are important none-the-less and should be taken seriously.

Hit the Sack

Believe me, I understand that college is a crazy time and that there is a lot going on and schedules change constantly. Your mind may understand this but your body doesn't, so it needs a chance to recover from the daily exertion of your activities. You may not always be able to have a set routine from day to day but try to get at least 7-8 hours of sleep within a 24 hour period, whenever this may be. You might have to catch a nap in the morning or afternoon on certain days if that is the only free time you have. Getting proper rest is vital to your academic performance as well as your overall health.

Supplements - Not a Dirty Word

As discussed earlier, your new diet may not include the daily recommended allowances of fruits, vegetables and other necessary nutrients. Now would be a great time to start taking some type of vitamin if you never have before. There are plenty of kinds of vitamins out there all promising different benefits but EVERYBODY should at least be taking a basic daily multivitamin to provide you with essential vitamins and nutrients. They will help keep you from becoming sick as easily and will add to your overall general good health. A lot of you will be exposed to dozens and even hundreds of new people on a daily basis and this means millions of germs. I'm not saying supplements will save you from everything out there but they will sure help.

> *Quick Tip –*
> *The field of nutrition and health can be quite confusing to beginners, which is why many companies provide pre-packaged vitamin and supplement packs for you. This helps to simplify things by taking the guess work out of it.*

In addition, if you take prescription medications, make sure you take them as prescribed! The hectic pace of your new life may cause you to forget to stay on schedule but you must remember to take your meds. You need to take them for a reason and they are meant to help you.

College Stinks – Oh, No It Doesn't, But Maybe You Do?

Practicing good personal hygiene is another tip that should go without saying but it amazes me how many people still fall short in this category. Shower at least once a day, brush your teeth, and use deodorant. These seem like basic responsibilities, but they can get lost in the hustle and bustle of a busy schedule. Your necessary routines need to be attended to on a daily basis to stay clean and healthy. Not to mention that if you want other people to be around you for any extended period of time, you have to be tolerable!

A Clean House is a Happy House

Maintaining high sanitation levels in areas like the bathrooms and kitchens will help you to avoid sicknesses. These areas are the most common places for germs to live and multiply. Use clean rags and disinfectant sprays to properly kill these germs. Also remember not to leave out any food for an extended period of time that may spoil. Vacuum your floors and wash your sheets on a regular basis. Keeping these areas and items clean

> ***Reminder –***
> *Diligently keeping up with simple household tasks keeps sanitation levels high. Procrastination, in contrast, keeps these levels low.*

will limit or kill bacteria and other diseases that want to grow. The key here is doing your housework on a regular basis. Doing little things often will save you from having to clean up a big mess later. In addition to the health benefits of keeping your new home clean, there is an undeniably added bonus that a nicely kept place will have on your mental well-being.

Activate

We may not all be triathletes training for Iron Man competitions, but keeping a regularly scheduled exercise routine will help you to maintain a healthy body, improve your body image (which improves your mental well-being too) and produce a body that is stronger and more resistant to sickness and injuries.

Almost every school I know of has some sort of facility where you are able to exercise, and usually it's free. Even if you have never worked out before and aren't a huge fan of exercise, spending only a half hour a day four or five times a week at the gym will help tremendously.

> **Quick Tip –**
> *To help keep you motivated and your routine consistent, work out with a partner.*

If you are already an active person and like sports, many schools have intramural or club sports programs where you might find something you enjoy. These programs are a great way to get in shape and stay active. If traditional sports aren't your cup of tea, or you are just trying to expand your horizons, many of you will have opportunities to experience alternative exercise activities at your institution that you may have never been exposed to. Examples include rock climbing, fencing, water polo, rugby, archery, and much much more depending on the college you attend. At some places you can participate in these activities as a class and get a P.E. credit for them.

Every Day and in Every Way . . .

Using these seemingly simple, but often forgotten tips can help you achieve a greater sense of mental and physical well-being which will help you tremendously in many ways including, but not limited to, your success in school and your overall happiness. They may also help keep you from getting sick so that you don't miss out on class time or social activities.

Living a life as stress free as possible will keep you in a good mood and will allow you to spend your energy on the important things. Following these tips can make a world of difference to you if you are not currently practicing them. Bad habits are contagious and spread quickly if you aren't paying attention. Basic personal health practices are important and if neglected will result in undesirable consequences.

So be healthy, be happy, and make sure you remember that the little things do matter!

Watch for Symptoms of Stress

Change in Appetite, Nervousness, Irritability, Tension, Lack of Energy, Mood Swings, Loss of Sleep

2 Academics

Now on to the reason you are here in the first place, your higher education. Some even say this is the most important aspect of the college experience, although come Friday night that is debatable! But I digress.

You go to school to take classes, and these classes, no matter how frivolous you may think they are, are required to get a degree. The key to getting a degree without being in school for a decade is doing things right the first time. Getting the grades you want in your classes isn't as hard as you would think but there are a few secrets to keep in mind while in pursuit of them.

Before you start classes you first need to know what to take. Colleges and universities offer multiple degree programs and choosing which one you want to pursue is a major decision (pun intended). A large number of students aren't sure early on of what they want to be or what they want to do in life. This is a common feeling among students so don't worry. Over the course of your academic career you will be drawn to certain areas that interest you. If you do know what you want to do right off the bat that's great! I always tell people to chase their dreams and do something they know they will be happy at. A wise man once said, do what you love and you will never work a day in your life.

With that being said I want you to not only survive but to succeed in life so you might hear your parent's voice as I tell you that not all degrees are created equal. For example, generally a degree in Petroleum Engineering has far more earning potential than does a degree in Art History. We all know that money ain't the end all and be all of life, however a nice compromise might be to major in the more promising money making degree and minor in the art degree. That way, in the future you will be able to afford to invest in the historical art that you love! If you are dead set on a certain degree, no matter what it is, take a step back and think about it and your long term plans thoroughly before you begin.

You do vastly different things with different degrees so I want you to do your research beforehand to make sure you examine the future possibilities of the degree that you are trying to attain. Do not make a poor choice and end up not loving what you majored in because you may find yourself unhappy with your new career and will have wasted valuable time and money along the way. Visualize your future. Weigh the pros and cons of the degrees you are contemplating. Make your decision based on what will best equip you for your future career and simultaneously maximize your happiness.

Questions To Ponder...

1. How long will it take me to earn this degree?
2. Is this degree feasible for me money-wise and difficulty-wise?
3. Exactly what jobs will I be qualified for with this degree?
4. How much future money am I realistically looking at making?
5. Where will I be able to live and work when I have this degree?
6. Does this degree provide for future flexibility in the ever-changing job market?

Next is a chart based on a recent 2012 Forbes.com ranking of the best and worst college majors. Note these rankings are based on earnings, job opportunities, and unemployment rates.[2] [3]

As you observe you can see that the "hard sciences" are well represented on the left side of the graph. That is not to say you won't ever be successful if you have a degree in music or art, all it says is that on average the engineering and science degrees are more "valuable". Again, this all depends on your definition of valuable. Just something to think about...

---

[2] Goudreau, Jenna. "The 10 Worst College Majors." Forbes. 11 October 2012. 27 December 2012.
http://www.forbes.com/sites/jennagoudreau/2012/10/11/the-10-worst-college-majors/
[3] Goudreau, Jenna. "The 15 Most Valuable College Majors." Forbes. 15 May 2012. 27 December 2012.
http://www.forbes.com/sites/jennagoudreau/2012/05/15/best-top-most-valuable-college-majors-degrees/

Best College Majors

- Biomedical Engineering
- Biochemistry
- Computer Science
- Software Engineering
- Environmental Engineering
- Civil Engineering
- Geology
- Management Information Systems
- Petroleum Engineering
- Applied Mathematics

Worst College Majors

- Fine Arts
- Anthropology/Archaeology
- Commercial Art and Graphic Design
- History
- Film, Video, and Photographic Arts
- Philosophy and Religious Studies
- Liberal Arts
- Music
- English Language and Literature
- Physical Fitness and Parks Recreation

Now even if you haven't settled on a specific degree hopefully you have decided on at least the general field of study you want to dive into. Early on it can be smart to leave your options open, especially if you aren't quite sure on what exactly it is you want to do when you graduate, but try to at least start your education in the general field of study that you are interested in even if it is fairly broad. By exposing yourself to one main area of study and having a large group of individual areas underneath it you can better expose yourself to a larger job market when you graduate. In a university setting that means picking the right college.

An example of this is if you enroll in the college of business, you would be able to major in accounting, marketing, finance, management, economics, etc.

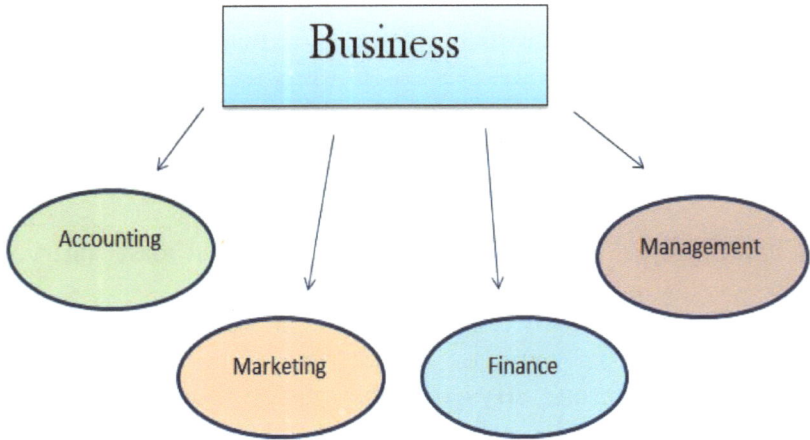

After a couple of semesters exploring different options, and taking the basic required classes you will most likely be able to narrow down your choice of degree and will be drawn to a specialty that stands out to you.

The point I am trying to make is that wasted time is wasted money. It is important to have a basic idea of where you want to be

> ### *Quick Tip -*
> *For those with conflicted thoughts about similar degrees, keep your options open as long as possible by taking classes that will meet requirements for multiple degrees until you can no longer do so. This will buy you time and will still keep you on track to graduate on time.*

and what you want to do. All universities have multiple colleges and by choosing a field of study that will be consistent with your interests, skill sets, and knowledge base you will save time, money, and effort in the long run. Nobody wants to have to start over from scratch halfway through their college career.

Changes in L-Attitudes

For many of you, the college you will be attending is going to be an unfamiliar place. Even if you have not moved far from home, or you know the city or town where the school is located, this doesn't mean you know the layout of the campus.

After you have your schedule and know what your classes are I highly recommend if you have free time before school starts to take a visit to the campus to get a better sense of where you are and where you will need to be going. This may be an easier task for some of you if your campus isn't very big but sometimes they can be spread out all over town and you want to be prepared.

First, how are you getting to school? Transportation can be a major issue at many schools because of the large volume of people the institution has to accommodate. I encourage you to decide how you will be getting to and from school and classes. Finding out if you have to walk, drive, bike, or take a shuttle will save you time and trouble. Next look at your schedule and search out the individual classrooms you will be sitting in. Your classes may be on different floors and in different buildings so do a little investigating and find out where you will need to be. By knowing where to go beforehand you can avoid the problems of the more unprepared students. Also, it would be smart to find out locations of the different common areas and facilities. This includes student unions, cafeterias, libraries, gyms, and any other area that will be useful to you.

To recap – the secret to being happy after college is to get the degree that you want. The secret to getting that degree is to pass the classes that are required in the shortest period of time. Just passing your classes and getting a degree with average grades is often not enough in this day and age. The job market for college grads is highly competitive and just because you have a piece of paper that says you have a degree doesn't make you any more special than somebody else with that same piece of paper from the same or another school. You need to develop special properties to make you stand out from the crowd. One of these properties can be your GPA. Having a respectable GPA in college may be much harder to accomplish than it was for you in high school. These next tips I will give you were key for me in my academic journey.

Making the Grade

Meeting the Prof.

Make a point to introduce yourself to your professors and do this early on in the semester so that they will remember you and you will not get lost in the crowd. Also, visit your professors during their office hours even if you don't need help. Just being able to make small talk with a professor shows them you are interested in them and therefore their class. Professors are people too and who doesn't like a little attention? If you do need help with schoolwork obviously this is a smart decision. It shows your professors that you care about your grades and are proactive about getting good ones. They will take note of this and are more likely remember your name when they are grading papers. Heck, if they like you they may even cut you some slack when it comes to the more subjective aspects of their grading. In short, be a person to your professor, not a number.

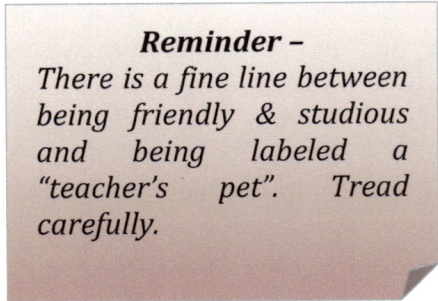

Reminder –
There is a fine line between being friendly & studious and being labeled a "teacher's pet". Tread carefully.

Notables

Take notes. I know this can seem monotonous but oftentimes you don't have to take very extensive notes because many times the professor already has printouts, puts them online, or keeps them on a PowerPoint presentation. With that being said, at the very least make sure you are taking an outline of your professor's lecture. If nothing else, this helps keep you engaged in class and it puts whatever subject you are learning about on your mind. This also helps keep you off of your smartphones or other distracting devices.

Find Your Dojo

A huge key in being able to understand the material you study and actually learn from it is having the ability to focus. When you are doing your homework or reading from a textbook or whatever your studying entails make sure you have a quiet place to go that has no distractions. Your room, a computer lab, or my favorite place, the library, can all be useful. Find whatever works for you personally. Having a distraction free learning environment is a key to your focus and your focus is a key to your studying success.

Measure Twice Cut Once

Periodically (a couple of times a week), look over the past readings or homework assignments for your class to make sure you

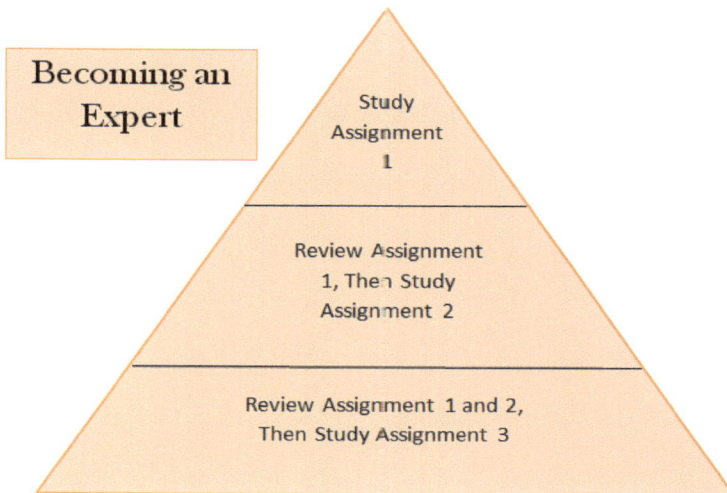

Becoming an Expert

Study Assignment 1

Review Assignment 1, Then Study Assignment 2

Review Assignment 1 and 2, Then Study Assignment 3

have a handle on the information. Many classes are based on information that builds on itself, so make sure that you understand the first few lessons because a lot of times the information you need to know in the future lessons directly correlates to what the previous ones have taught. This helps you from ever getting too far behind in your studies.

Study Buddies

Try to find a good support system of classmates that you can study with. Most likely everyone is in the same boat as you and is just as nervous or confused about the class as you are. Try to find a few students who you think want to do well and succeed in the class and then schedule a time where you can all get together and study. Depending on your options, be picky when you are choosing these classmates. Avoid slackers who won't be useful in a study session but also avoid those who know the material completely. Often times these students will not study hard because frankly, they don't have to, and they will be just as useless for you as studying with a slacker.

Use Your Lifelines

If you are struggling with a certain topic or class, reach out to find alternatives. Your school, or clubs or honoraries within the school, will most likely have some sort of tutoring program available to you and it is often free. There are also different types of study sessions or after-hours help courses that can be found on

campuses. I strongly recommend that you pursue these options if you need a little extra help or just want to get ahead and ace the course. Ask

> **Reminder –**
> *The entire purpose of tutoring programs and study sessions is to help you out! If you need the help take advantage of it.*

an advisor or mentor for help to find out where these programs for your school are located.

Take This Class And Cram It!

For your exams that is, not as a replacement for diligently studying all semester, but as another tool to use so that all the information you need to know is fresh on your mind at the time of the exam. I find it very useful to look over notes or read my textbooks for a few hours before I have an exam because the repetition of looking at everything over and over ingrains it into my mind and I remember it better once the test starts. I would also do this the night before your test because your brain will continue to process and think about the information all while you sleep. What could be easier?

Cash In On Extra Credit

When given opportunities to perform extra credit assignments you should ALWAYS take advantage of them. Oftentimes the extra credit assignments your professors will provide aren't as hard as your normal assignments, so why not participate? By taking a little bit of extra time and effort you can cash in on a higher grade than you would have otherwise received. Again, this also shows your professors that you are willing to go above and beyond to get the grade you want and believe me, they definitely notice.

Winning the Paper Chase

You need to take your studies and your future seriously, so use these tips to help you achieve the high scores you want. Oftentimes students' grades will slip precipitously from what they were used to in high school due to any number of reasons, but if you put these tips to use you will avoid many of those problems. Try to have an absolutely awesome time in college, but remember your education is at stake, and you or somebody you know, is paying good money to have you succeed. School is your current "number one job" so do it well.

This is one of those times where you need to pay attention to the details during your studies because classes can quickly get out of hand if you are not mindful of

> **Quick Tip –**
> *Time management is an extremely important part of succeeding in your academics. To most effectively prioritize your schedule make sure you do the more heavily weighted assignments and/or the ones with the earliest due dates before the others.*

them. Use these tips to succeed and don't dig yourself into a hole early in your academic career because it will be twice as hard to dig yourself out of later. Mistakes in studying compound exponentially so follow these easy and simple steps to help you succeed in the classroom.

3   Social Life

O nce you have a handle on your class schedule, you can move on to developing an equally important aspect of college - your social life. Everybody wants to go off to college and have a great time while there. For many this is the first time away from their parents and there is an amazing amount of new-found freedom during these years. Learning how to properly manage this freedom and get the most out of college is one of the hardest balancing acts there is. We have all heard stories of students who party too hard and dropout of college after only their first semester or two. At the other extreme, nobody wants to be the loner who doesn't have any fun when you should be out having the best experiences of your life. Here are a few tips to follow to ensure you are not on either extreme end of the spectrum.

Get Out There!

The first step in having a successful social life is to be social! It all starts with getting out there and exposing yourself to the college lifestyle. One of the easiest ways to do this is by having friends who are already at the same school as you. This is a great starting point and a network you should rely on, but this should not be the end all and be all of your social experience. College isn't about hanging out with your high school friends and doing the same things you did with them in high school. However, your old friends can be a great help to you in plugging into your new social life. Get together, go out, and have fun but do not limit your "group" to just old friends.

College is a totally different place and to maximize your experience you have to get out and meet new people. Looking back down the long corridor of time, it very well may be these new people who will become your oldest friends. This is the best opportunity that you will ever have to reinvent yourself, so make the most of it!

Damned Glad to Meet You

For dorm dwellers, meeting and greeting the people on your floor or in your wing is a natural place to start. Usually there are mandatory meetings that you will all be together for. This can be a perfect opportunity to start a conversation with somebody new. Dorms are active people hubs and even just passing by somebody in the halls can be a great opportunity to "meet and greet". Most times you will also have one or more roommates. Not only will you get to know your roommates but many times their friends become your new friends.

For those who live off campus or live in an apartment or townhouse you will have to work a bit harder, but don't fret, you aren't out of luck. Again, a great place to start is by already having friends you room with or go to school with, but even if you don't, this shouldn't be a problem. There are plenty of other places to fraternize with your fellow students.

Most schools have common areas with places to eat, study, or participate in recreational activities while killing time before or after class. Take advantage of these places. There should be a big enough volume of people and activities here to satisfy your social appetite.

Meet the Greek

Speaking of fraternizing, plenty of people find many lasting friendships in fraternities and sororities. The "Greeks" (so called because they use Greek letters to identify their different houses e.g. ΔΔΔ= Delta Delta Delta Sorority) make it easy! Go to rush week, meet a ton of people, and see if you like the men and women at the different houses. Pledge if one strikes your fancy. The Greek system is all about organized social interaction and scholarly pursuits. Being in a fraternity or sorority is not for everyone but just giving it a shot won't hurt anything.

Join the Club

If you are interested in a particular subject, most universities have many different clubs that you can join and many of these clubs are directly linked to your particular major or minor area of study, adding academic value to your social life. As discussed earlier, if sports are your thing, many schools have all kinds of intramural or even club sports to play. Being on a team is a great way to get to know people and make connections. If you want to look into these clubs there should be help desks scattered around your campus with all the information you need to get started.

Popular Club & Intramural Sports

- Baseball
- Cycling
- Rugby
- Hockey
- Frisbee
- Water Polo
- Skiing
- Volleyball
- Soccer
- Track
- Badminton
- Bowling
- Basketball

Various Student Organizations and Clubs

- *Environmental Clubs*
- *Student Government*
- *Foreign Language Clubs*
- *Fraternities and Sororities*
- *Book Clubs*
- *Science Clubs*
- *Business Clubs*
- *Student Political Organizations*

Begin at the Beginning

If you are attending a university, most likely your class sizes will be substantially larger than they were for you in high school. This can seem a little overwhelming at first but start by making small talk with the students you sit next to, or even better if you are assigned to a study group with a few other people, try to engage with them. More likely than not they are just as nervous as you are and it would make that person feel much better if somebody took the pressure off of him or her by engaging that person in a light conversation.

Again, it may seem a little daunting and intimidating to talk to somebody you have never met, but YOU need to be the catalyst of YOUR social journey. You can start a conversation by saying something about the class you're in, the homework assignment that was due, if they went to the game or not, or if they know where a certain place on campus is located.

Don't go into a conversation expecting to find the love of your life or your future best friend. Understand that this is just a starting point for you in your social journey. If things don't go well, so what? It was one person you didn't know and you now have more experience meeting people under your belt. The more you practice anything the better you will be at it and this is true of being sociable as well.

Initiate. Be the person who gets things done. Don't be that person who sits on the sidelines waiting to be engaged. Remember this is your new start so, well, get started.

Your Expanding Universe

The key to building and expanding upon your social life depends in part upon social etiquette. By social etiquette I mean the way in which you conduct yourself in public places during a social experience. Yes, even in college there are rules. If you ever want invited back to somebody's house, or to an event, you must be able to sell yourself as somebody who is worthy of the invitation. To properly accomplish this when invited to any sort of gathering there are a few simple tips to follow that can make you stand out from the crowd, in a good way.

Where Are Your Manners?

Be Prepared

Understand the type of event you are attending and prepare yourself accordingly. Wear the proper attire and understand what will be

> **Reminder –**
> *Dress for the occasion. Don't be that guy who shows up to a formal party in a t-shirt and jeans.*

happening at the occasion that you choose to attend.

Be Thoughtful

I am not talking about being thoughtful in the sense of being kind, although that is important too. Rather, before an event you need to be mindful of who you will be with, what you will be doing, and what you will be talking about. A great outing oftentimes doesn't "just happen", so you need to think beforehand and be at least marginally prepared for who you will see and what you will say. By doing this you will reduce your risk of awkward moments and slow nights. Treat it somewhat like a class. Study beforehand, prepare, and even develop conversation starters.

Be Gracious and Generous

When you are invited to an event or a party, try to make it a point early on in the night to find the host of your shindig and thank him or her for the invite. Also, depending on the occasion

> **Reminder –**
> *Money is (usually) tight for everybody, so don't be a cheapskate who mooches off the group.*

you should always bring a little something, be it food or drink, to add to the mix. A little donation of money is always appreciated. It all depends on the event, but you don't want to be remembered as the freeloader at the party who did not contribute and ate or drank everything in sight.

Never Stand Out BUT Make Yourself Known

By this I mean you never want to be somebody who is annoying, overbearing, or too blasted or wild, because that is a surefire way to never get an invite back. On the other hand, you do

> **Reminder –**
> *"Lampshade on top of the dome" never has been, nor will be a flattering look.*

not want to be the awkward wall-flower. You want to be social enough to have an engaging conversation with multiple people, join in on any games or activities, and be remembered, but in a good way.

Know Your Limits

College is a time where you will be exposed to things you have never had or tried before. Being adventurous and trying new things is generally a good thing but you must know your limits when it comes to certain areas, especially alcohol or drugs. If you do not know your limits there could be negative consequences including getting sick, embarrassing yourself, showing up on social media (in a bad way), and the ever present danger of legal troubles as well. If you don't know your limits, always err on the side of caution until you learn what you can handle. Start out slowly if you are uncertain of what to expect.

Avoid illegal drugs as the negative ramifications are exponentially worse. Some offenses that might be treated as citations or misdemeanors when committed using alcohol may very well be treated as felonies if committed using illegal drugs, so be more than careful. You are starting your adult life here so don't start it out with a criminal record.

Know When to Leave

We have all been in situations when you know that the evening is winding down but there is just that one person or couple who seem to be oblivious to the fact that the night is coming to a close and they stay way past their welcome. You do not want to be remembered as one of these people and this is something that you just have to learn to judge based on how the night is

> **Reminder –**
> When guests overstay their welcome it can be quite annoying for the host. Be aware of your surroundings.

flowing. Every situation is different but if you are mindful of your surroundings you should be able to know when it is time to leave. College all-nighters should USUALLY be reserved for studying, not partying.

Re-Thank Your Host

Sometimes once is enough but if you had a good experience, or really want to have another one with these people sometime in the future, make sure to re-approach the host of the party and thank them again for the great time you had before you depart.

> ***Quick Tip –***
> *Before you head out ask your host if you can do anything to help to cleanup. Even if they say no, your gesture will be remembered. If they say yes, roll up your sleeves and have a good time.*

All Things in Moderation

The biggest key by far in any social setting is to exercise moderation in all things. Being able to find a happy medium in your comings and goings is a trait that is much appreciated, and believe me, people notice. Knowing when to keep a joke going, when and how to properly start and finish a conversation, when you have had enough to drink, and when it's time to leave a situation all fall under this category. Moderation is a skill that can save you a lot of trouble (socially and legally) and will also make you quite popular in the long run. It is a skill that is perfected over time and is learned when you get to truly know yourself, your attributes, and your limits. Where better to develop moderation than college?

Drinking 101

The first thing I would like to say on this subject is that drinking is NOT a mandatory sport you are forced to participate in just because you are in college. If you don't drink, you should never feel pressured to join in. Being a non-drinker is a fine choice. It is a less expensive option, and you can always use the time you save by not drinking doing something more productive, like studying. With that being said, I understand that many of you will not fall into this category and will be making drinking a part of your college experience. A few brave souls may even make it somewhat of a pastime!

Some of you would-be college drinkers may have never been exposed to alcohol before. If so, then this will be a new experience for you. On the other hand, some of you may already be fairly seasoned in the art of drinking. It doesn't matter which category you fall under, there are a certain immutable rules about booze.

You may start by asking the question "Are all alcoholic beverages created equal?" The answer is NO they are not, and I am not just talking about the process of making different kinds of alcohol, their tastes, and the bottles they come in.

Alcohol production is a very technical and interesting field so if you are intrigued and want to learn more about it I would recommend you research the process. Right now I am more concerned with your social life and helping you understand a few key points about alcohol consumption.

The first thing you should understand when drinking is a word called "proof". Every alcohol has a proof. Generally it's printed right on the front of the bottle. The word proof refers to the percentage of alcohol in the drink. The higher the proof, the higher the amount of alcohol in the drink which means you will need less of it to become intoxicated. Beer, wine, and adult teas/lemonades will generally have a fairly lower alcohol content (ranging from about 4%-20%) than your typical "spirits" or "hard liquor" (e.g. whiskeys, vodkas, and rums). Hard alcohols normally range from between 35% to 60% alcohol which is 70 to 120 proof. It is possible to find some liquor that has an even higher alcohol content. This is something very important to keep in mind when deciding what to drink.

Also keep in mind that you cannot necessarily judge how much alcohol is in a drink by its taste. Many a hung over college student has found out the hard way that the punch that tasted like fruit juice was loaded with copious amounts of Everclear, vodka, rum, and anything else that the host or their guests decided to add during the course of the evening.

Your B.A.C. (blood alcohol concentration) is the scientific term used to describe your level of intoxication. The higher your B.A.C. the more intoxicated you are. In most states you are considered legally intoxicated if your B.A.C is at .08 or higher. That means that 8/100 of 1% of the blood in your system is actually alcohol. So, you see it doesn't take much for one to be considered legally drunk. Here is a handy Wikipedia link on the subject: http://en.wikipedia.org/wiki/Blood_alcohol_content.

The B.A.C. scale works the same for everyone but the effects of one's drinking can appear very different for different

> **Quick Tip –**
> General understanding is that it takes one hour for your body to fully process 1 shot, 1 beer, or 1 glass of wine.

people. For example you and a friend may have had exactly the same amount of alcohol in the same setting and at the same time but one of you may appear much more intoxicated than the other. Why is this?

Many factors influence B.A.C. including age, weight, sex, gender, and even genetics. Everybody is affected differently when it comes to drinking, so if you choose to drink, it is very important to find your limits. Now, the only way to learn your limits is through experience, but there are ways to make sure to keep your drinking experiences under the "enjoyable" category and not the "freaky" category.

Being able to properly handle yourself in a social situation where alcohol is present is crucial to developing your skills in public if you are going to be a drinker. Here are a few tips that beginners and veterans alike should use when planning on drinking:

Chow Down

Always eat a meal before you drink. Having food on your stomach is very important when you plan on drinking. Without a meal beforehand to help metabolize the liquor in your stomach you may find yourself significantly affected by only a small amount of alcohol.

BYOB (Be Your Own Bartender)

Make your own drinks. If you are not drinking out of prepackaged bottles or cans, and drinks are being made in cups, if at all possible, take charge and pour your own.

> **Reminder –**
> *"eye-balling it" and "guesstimating" may not be the most accurate way to pour drinks.*

This will allow you to see exactly what and how much of something you are consuming.

Slipping a Mickey

We have all heard of "date rape" drugs being slipped into women's drinks, and the fact of the matter is that it does happen. So, ladies, keep an eye on your Solo cup.

Stat Tracker

Keep track of how many beverages you consume. Don't lose count of how much you have had to drink because this can lead to an overconsumption and may very well send you into a highly intoxicated state.

> **Quick Tip –**
> *Keep a count of your intake. If your drink is served with a piece of fruit, keep track of how many you have had by the number of pieces in your glass. You can also use swizzle sticks, bottle tops, or anything else, but use something.*

Keepin' It Real

Avoid peer pressure when drinking in large groups. Everybody has a different limit and some people can handle a lot more alcohol than others. Don't get caught up in trying to out-do or impress someone. If you aren't very experienced or can't handle your alcohol very well your attempt to impress could completely backfire and you will end up looking very bad indeed. Drinking games are often included in a party so be careful because it is very easy to over indulge in these situations. It is better to take yourself out of the game too early rather than too late.

H_2O

Drink water throughout the night. Drinking alcohol dehydrates your body and by drinking water you will not only keep your body hydrated that night, but you will feel better the next day. Drinking water will help keep your B.A.C. lower than it would be without. Water helps to thin-out, or dilute, the contents of whatever is in your stomach and it slows the pace of your drinking. So, alternate between an adult beverage and a glass of water.

The Tortoise Always Wins

Learn how to pace yourself throughout the night. Treat the night like a marathon, not a sprint, and do not consume copious amounts of alcohol in a short span of time. You may not realize it at first, but even if you do not get sick, your body cannot process all of the alcohol in your system at once. It will eventually hit you hard and will probably end your night prematurely.

Enough about Booze

Developing great social skills is like anything else, they are LEARNED traits acquired through practice and experience. Despite what you may think about that insufferably popular cheerleader back in high school, people are not born with naturally perfect social skills. Don't worry if you didn't have the greatest social graces in high school because you are now in a completely different phase of your life. Remember, the people who are socially successful have made the mistakes already and have learned from them. The social strategies discussed in this chapter will help you to get out there, gain experience, and meet many new people which will inevitably lead to a great social life and help you become the person that you want to be.

The more people you know, the more parties, gatherings, and events you will be invited to attend. In the long run you will make some of your best friends, and meet people who will be very influential to your future.

If you are naturally an apprehensive or cautious person, don't be afraid to be a little more outgoing and push your comfort zone outward. College is a new chapter in your life. It's a time where you can start over and reinvent yourself. You may not believe me until you experience it, but your college years are totally different than anything you have gone through up to this point. This can be your fresh start or just a time to re-invent yourself. These are the years of your life where you truly find yourself and become the person you will be for the rest of your life.

Meeting new people and adding them to the friends you already have is a recipe for a very fun time, and everyone knows a well-rounded college experience cannot be considered complete without a few crazy stories. So get out there, learn a lot along the way, and just have fun!

4   Culture Shock

nother important consideration in your college life is the huge change that will likely take place in your living arrangements. A dorm, apartment, townhouse, fraternity or sorority house, or wherever you may live is going to be a big change from how you were living back home. This means much more freedom and to quote a Spiderman movie, "With great power comes great responsibility" Regardless of your dwelling place, here are some things to remember to have a fun and rewarding living situation.

If you are moving to a completely new city to go to school, one of the first things you should do is to discover the town. Go out and explore the place, visit the downtown area, find out where people your age hang out, and find places that you know will interest you. Getting your bearings will help make the transition into your new life that much easier. You may find a great restaurant or shopping area that you would like to frequent.

Becoming comfortable with your surroundings will create a sense of home, because let's face it, this <u>IS</u> your home for the time being so make it yours!

Keeping Your Landlord Happy

If you are not living at home, then most of you will be renting or leasing the place you will live. This includes apartments, houses, and yes even dorm rooms.

Renting means you do NOT own the place and must abide by your landlord's rules. Make sure that from the beginning you have a very clear understanding of what is and what is not allowed in your place of residence. Knowing what you can and cannot do beforehand will save you from future fights, future stress, and can save you some of that elusive stuff we call money. First impressions are everything and if at all possible I strongly urge you to get off on the right foot with your landlord from the very beginning and then keep it that way.

Pay Up

You must remember the due dates for your rent and utility payments and pay accordingly. This is a pretty basic rule but if you don't take this one seriously a bad situation with your landlord will definitely arise. Being known as one of your landlord's responsible tenants can only make it easier for you now and in the future, when a potential new landlord calls asking for a recommendation from your old landlord.

Follow the Rules

Simple enough right? Make sure you know what you are able to do before you do it. Do not make modifications to the residence without knowing if it is allowed under the terms of the lease. Do not have a party if the fine print in your lease says you can't. Carefully read over your lease agreement. Remember, a

> **Quick Tip –**
> Oftentimes larger schools will have an attorney available for students to consult. You may want to take advantage of this service and have them take a look at your lease before you sign it.

lease is a binding contract and breaking a contract intentionally or accidentally can lead to legal troubles that may follow you long after college is over.

Ask Questions

You should always ask your landlord for permission if you are uncertain about something. If at any point you need to ask your landlord a question, he or she will appreciate that you asked and should give you a prompt answer. Your landlord will think highly of you if you act like a thoughtful person who thinks before he acts. He or she would much rather have you ask beforehand if you can paint the walls pink rather than afterwards. Again this is all about building a good relationship.

Keep It Classy

Usually your landlord reserves the right to come over and inspect the place whenever he or she pleases. Therefore you want your home picked up and presentable, inside and out, at all times. It is much easier to clean up small clutter often rather than to procrastinate and leave a giant mess for later. It always seems like the one time you do have a big mess is exactly the time when your landlord drops by for a surprise inspection. To be safe and avoid an unhappy visit just keep your home clean on a regular basis.

Compliments NOT Complaints

Try to be cordial with the people you live next to. It is a good idea to introduce yourself early on and try to get things off on the right foot from the beginning. If you are going to throw a party or have people over it is always courteous to let your neighbors know beforehand that there might be some extra noise or activity. And if you like them, invite them over!

Even if you don't end up liking your landlord and you don't see eye to eye, always remember that they hold most of the cards and because you are renting from them you have to abide by their rules. I am not saying that their opinion is always right, but they own the property and you do not. Be cautious any time you sign an agreement with anyone and make sure you read over your lease carefully before you sign to make sure that you will be able to be governed by their rules and make it work. Don't agree to anything if you will not be able to keep up your end of the bargain.

Keeping the Peace

Now on to an equally important aspect of your new life – roommates. I predict that almost every one of you will have at least one roommate at some point during your college career. Even if you have the means to go it alone throughout your college days, I would encourage you to take on one or more roommates. Learning how to deal with other people in a very personal setting is something you may not have had to deal with before but it is a very important skill to master. It does not matter if you are living with somebody you have never met or a friend you have known all your life. There are certain rules you should abide by to make a successful living arrangement work. Here are a few things you can do to make your time with your roomies run more smoothly.

Going by the Book

The very first thing you need to do with your roommates is sit down and have a meeting to discuss and make various house rules. This step will save countless future problems from ever arising.

Understand that you and your roommates are all different people who all have different backgrounds, experiences, attitudes, feelings, and beliefs. You have to respect everybody in the house when making these rules and everyone will have to compromise about various issues to come to a consensus.

These rules need to cover a wide range of topics such as how you will pay bills, how food is bought and eaten, what is and is not allowed in certain areas of the house, what is and is not shared, when and how the cleaning will be done, who and when people are allowed over, etc. This needs to be a thorough and wide ranging conversation. Make sure you have a

Reminder-
Obviously certain issues can't be controlled or fixed by a rule. But any area of dispute should be brought up regardless. At least the issue is out there and everybody knows that it might become a subject of contention. This way nobody is surprised when it comes up later.

clear and concise understanding when you are done talking. Finally, write these rules down so everybody knows at all times what they are, and they can be updated or amended as needed.

House Rules

1. Sunday - deep clean house, team effort
2. Keep common areas picked up
3. Keep personal items in rooms
4. No guests after midnight on weekdays
5. Split cost of utility bills
6. Ration food out evenly

Dispute Resolution

My parents are both attorneys so I have learned more than a few times about conflict resolution. They tell me that every contract they write includes a dispute resolution clause. This clause anticipates that there will be problems that will likely arise between the parties. Therefore, while the parties are still on amicable terms that is the time to agree on how disputes will be resolved between them. Roommates should do the same thing. Lay the ground rules for resolving problems in advance of them popping up.

Communication is Key

Even with a clear set of rules problems will likely arise among roommates. This is just a fact of life. The easiest way to deal with problems is a face to face talk with the other person. When I say face to face, I don't mean Facebook to Facebook! Don't air your dirty laundry in public. Instead present your issues to your roommate in a calm and clear manner. Really listen to what he or she has to say about the situation and try to see things from his or her point of view. If you act in a civil manner towards one another you can almost always expect things to work out.

Find a way to compromise with the other person so that you both end up benefiting. Do not let problems go unaddressed or let important issues slide. This only creates more tension and what were once unhappy situations can turn into toxic ones very quickly. Problems, like infections, fester if ignored. Be up front with your roommates and stop problems the moment they happen. There are few things worse than having to live with somebody you are upset with. Talk it out!

> **Quick Tip –**
> *If you find yourself in a heated argument with a roommate, it may be best to remove yourself from an escalating situation until things calm down and you are able to talk things out with a clear mind. When you are enraged, nothing that is said will be of any good and your problem will most likely get worse.*

The Golden Rule

In general, try to be as courteous as possible to your roommates. Don't do things that you wouldn't want done to you if you were on the receiving end. If you tell your roommate you will do something, do it. Keep your word and you will build trust. A great author whom I enjoy by the name of Richard J. Maybury puts it this way: There are two rules – (1.) Do what you say you are going to do; and (2.) Don't encroach upon others or their property.

Simple things like not hogging food, keeping your areas clean, and not making too much noise can go a long way to having a happy home. These are basic courtesies but the key is to pay attention to your roommates. You can usually see the signs when somebody is upset. Like Mr. Maybury says, "do not infringe on your roommate, his or her property, or his or her areas." Most often the house rules will be enough to deal with the majority of issues that arise, but over the course of the semester or the year, be mindful of your footprint, don't overstep your bounds, and try to put yourself in other people's shoes to see things from their perspective.

The Happy Life

Living in a new state, town, or even just a strange residence can be a big culture shock. When you are thrown outside your comfort zone you have to learn to make adjustments on the fly. By remembering the aforementioned tips and tricks of the trade you can avoid or solve most problems that you may encounter. The three important things to remember in surviving your new environmental changes are; try to keep your landlord happy, have a healthy relationship with your roommates, and become familiar with your local environment. The change in venue will be quite smooth if you are able to successfully accomplish these things.

5 Stretching Your Dollar

Most college students are a little on the broke side. No matter how much we have saved, what job we had in high school, or how many $2 bills our grandmother gave us in our birthday and holiday cards, we still don't seem to have enough money to pay for everything. If this describes you, you WILL have to live on a budget. Yeah, I know it's not ideal. This may be one of the poorest times in your life due to the expenses that you incur. But remember, the reason you are here is to get a good education so that you can do what you want, and live how you want, in the future that you create for yourself.

In addition to any scholarships that you have already scored, here a few money saving tips to stretch your dollar further so that you can live a little larger.

Money Saving Tips

It Pays to be a Student

It doesn't matter where you go to school, all colleges and universities will have all sorts of student discount programs available to you. It is your job to take advantage of them. As a student you can receive discounted, or even free services, encompassing a wide array of products and services. Examples include healthcare, recreation, software programs, tickets to events, cheap food, access to books and databases, free printing, school sponsored trips, and much more.

> ***Quick Tip –***
> *If you have a friend or roommate in the same class, you can save money by splitting the cost of an overpriced textbook by buying only one copy. You can share the same materials thereby saving you both half the cost.*

Every school is different and will offer different things; I challenge you to try to take advantage of each and every thing you possibly can!

Shop Local

The local businesses around your school understand they are in a college town and therefore they often market to the college population. This means many of them will provide students with discounts and periodic deals on all sorts of goods and services. Cheap movie tickets, dollar-slice pizza nights, and happy hours with free food buffets are just a few examples of the large market of discounted items you can find. In today's challenging retail market, most businesses, even the smallest among them, will offer discounts on their products for students. You can often get a good deal around town on lots of things that you need or want.

> **Reminder –**
> *Small business owners are always trying to find a way to keep up with the large national corporations. One way of holding onto their market share is to offer discounts to local niches (college students).*

Share the Burden

This means that when you have the opportunity to share the cost of something with someone else, do so. When you and your roommates need food, go to the store as a group and buy in bulk. When you checkout you can split the bill and in the end you will all save money.

Having your friends over to pitch-in for a grill night or for a giant pot of soup can be a great social experience and you can save a lot of money by eating at home. This is true for everything, not just food. Carpooling and the use of group discounts are all ways of sharing costs. The more people you have the cheaper it will be for everyone concerned. Your friends and fellow students need and want to save money too, so when you go out as a group be on the lookout for a way to share expenses that benefits everyone.

> **Reminder –**
> *Invite your friends over for dinner and ask them to bring a can of something to throw into a community pot. Hobo Stew, as it is known, can make for an interesting meal!*

DIY

If at all possible, do it yourself! You are in college now and will be faced with all sorts of home or car repair challenges, and every time you are able to meet and overcome one by yourself you are saving money and improving your skill set at the same time.

If the sink isn't working, or the lawnmower won't start, assess the situation and look at the problem thoroughly before paying to have it fixed. From my own personal experience, I can say that when a few college students get together and put a little effort into figuring something out, most of the time they can solve the problem and won't need to make the dreaded phone call to ask a parent for advice.

Even minor fixes around the house can cost hundreds of dollars if done by a professional, and by at least trying to do it yourself you have the opportunity to save a bundle of money. Handling minor problems

> **Reminder-**
> *Guys, you can score major brownie points with the girls if you can be the one who can find out why their car won't start or how to fix their appliances. Expand your skill set!*

without having to ask somebody for help will pay dividends for the rest of your life. Obviously, if something is serious or potentially dangerous you should ask a professional, but for the minor things, give yourself a shot at DIY and most of the time you will be pleasantly surprised with the positive results you achieve.

Get Tech Savvy

As a college student, 90+% of you will be using computers or special software programs in your classes. These things become quite pricey fast, but there are ways of stretching your tech dollar too.

One thing to know is that technology companies love students. They figure if they can get you hooked on their products in college that you will continue to use them for the rest of your life. To entice you, many, if not all of the big software and computer manufacturers have

> *Quick Tip-*
> *Microsoft, Apple, Google, and others sell full feature products at specially discounted student prices.*

"student bundles" to fully equip you for the high-tech part of your college career. Before you buy an operating system, or a computer, or another device check with the manufacturer or provider to see if they offer a student bundle. Generally, these bundles are fully functional programs or devices just as capable as their professional products offered to you at a fraction of the price. Also check to see what is available through your college or university. It pays to shop around.

When purchasing tech items on a limited budget it is important to keep in mind how to save as much money as possible all while getting the items you require. Here are three tech buying tips:

1. Set a budget <u>before</u> you go shopping. Many of us can be like kids in a candy store when exposed to all of the tantalizing choices that lay in front of us in an electronics store or online. When you create a budget of what you are willing to spend, and more importantly what you can afford to spend, you are able to limit your selections and narrow your options right off the bat, which makes the final purchase that much easier.

2. Determine the products you will need depending on your classes and their requirements. Do your research beforehand so that you will be prepared when classes start. If you do you will avoid making unnecessary purchases and will save money. Make a list of the programs and devices you NEED so that when it comes time for the salesperson to try to "upsell" you all types of add-ons or additional products you will not get suckered into spending money unnecessarily.

3. Ask what kind of bundles or deals are available at the different stores you shop in. Maybe you need a laptop, a printer, and a software package. Do not make your purchase at the first place you visit. To get the best deal it would be wise to shop around at a few different places, including online stores, to see which ones will give you the best price. Also be sure to ask if they know of any sales that are coming up in the near future. When you have done your research, exhausted your options, and found the best deal – THEN make your purchase.

After you have made your purchases, remember that most schools have dedicated IT departments to help their students. Oftentimes these IT departments will offer inexpensive, or even free, support services. Before you pay for help off campus, make sure to that those problems can't be resolved by your college's IT department.

The Other Side of the Coin

As valuable as it is for you to stretch your dollar and save money while at school, it can be even more rewarding to give back or to "pay it forward." And no, you don't have to donate a bunch of money or go on a peace mission to a faraway country to do it.

> **Reminder-**
> *Keep in mind that many charitable events can also be great social outings. Participating in a 5K or doing volunteer work with your friends can be rewarding on several different levels.*

There are endless things you can do to give to your local community and receive personal satisfaction at the same time. Your school will almost certainly have many charitable programs it supports. I encourage you to look into them and if you find one that you feel is worth participating in, join!

If you want to broaden your horizon outside of your college or university, you can help by simply keeping your eyes open to the needs of those around you. Keep in mind that opportunities are out there for you to help and make a difference in someone else's life. If you have spare time I recommend that you help out in any way that you can. Don't limit these years to strictly books and booze. This is a time when you may be in the best shape of your life and perhaps the last time that you have time and energy to give to others in a big way. I encourage you to use your youth and good health to help those around you who are not as blessed. There is whole world out there that needs help and every little thing you can do will help.

To Recap Money Matters

Living on a budget can be a new and difficult experience for many. Truth is, it isn't really that hard to save money if only you put a little bit of thought and effort into it. I hope you can use my tips to help you achieve your budget goals.

Learning to live on a budget means to live a little (or a lot) below your means. Knowing and employing this one little secret will serve you well now and well into the future. If you can use this secret to reduce or even eliminate your school debt, then you will be well on your way to a securing a successful future!

I hope you all graduate with great degrees and get well-paying jobs, or start successful businesses or practices, but by learning to budget and properly save money now you will already own the building blocks for your financial future. Again, let's not forget that giving back is just as important a lesson to learn as budgeting. So, use this time in your life to learn to better yourself in the aforementioned areas and you will become responsible and generous at the same time.

Conclusion

As you now know, college is a time of life where immense and fantastic changes happen. You will experience a myriad of new experiences, from your academic life to your night life to everything in-between. I hope most of them end up as good experiences! But it is how you deal with the bad experiences in life that will help you grow the most and will largely reflect your character. Why is it that professional sports teams often sign players that are twice as old and half as talented as young hotshots? It is due to the old timer's experience and character. The knowledge of the game and ability to perform well under stressful situations makes him a valuable member of the team. Developing this asset called experience and your simultaneously developing your character will be more valuable than any natural talent that you possess.

In college you will be hit with anything and everything and learning how to deal with all kinds of situations and problems will help you grow into the man or women you want to be. Don't be afraid to fail because there will be times when you will. Treat failure the same way that a scientist treats an experiment. According to science there are no failed experiments because you always learn something from every experiment regardless of result.

All I ask is that you enjoy your successes, that you learn from your mistakes, and that from both you grow as a person, even a little, each and every time so that by the end of your collegiate career you will be fully prepared for the life that is ahead of you!

From one student to another, I hope that you will find these tips helpful. Now it is up to you to go forth and be AMAZING…